The Hagopian Institute, LLC has compiled the *Idiom Junkie* series. The overall series includes over 5,000 idioms, focusing on a wide variety of idioms stretching from funny idioms, to necessary idioms, to rarely-used odd idioms. This particular edition of the series includes 500 idioms that will help you lead a more fulfilling life. This book is aimed at giving people positive idioms that will help inspire them to lead their lives in the right way. This will make an excellent coffee-table book for your guests to enjoy. Please share these idioms with your friends, family and co-workers.

Enjoy!

Todd Hagopian
President
The Hagopian Institute, LLC

a man's home is his castle
a man can do whatever he wants to in his own home

a stitch in time saves nine
if something needs to be done, do it right away, or the task is bound to get bigger and bigger

all roads lead to Rome
there are many ways to get something done

all the world's a stage
life is like a play, we merely go through the stages of our life acting our life out.

American as apple pie
person or thing having qualities that are seen as American, or U.S. specific

back to the drawing board
forced to start over

be there or be square
if you are not there, we will think you are not popular

beat a hasty retreat
to leave a place because it is dangerous or unpleasant

beauty is in the eye of the beholder

each person might define beauty or see things as beautiful depending on how they feel or what they prefer

better the devil you know

better to deal with the person you know, who you don't like, than to deal with someone you don't know who might be even worse

between the devil and the deep blue sea

deciding between two dangerous situations

big sky thinking

thinking about everything that might affect the situation, or thinking about something in a new way

bite your tongue
keep quiet

blow the cobwebs away
make room for new ideas

Bob's your uncle
easy from here on out

bounce back
to do well again after a bad loss

brainstorm
to think of as many new ideas or solution to a problem as possible

break the ice
start a conversation with a stranger, or in an uncomfortable situation

break the record
do something better than anyone ever has

break the silence
to talk when no one else is talking during an awkward silence

breathe a sigh of relief
to feel comfortable again after worrying about something

bright eyed and bushy tailed
to be full of energy and eager to do things

bring home the bacon
earn a living, make money, or be successful

bring off something
to succeed at something

bring the house down
to make people laugh or clap very loudly

bring to a close
to finish something

brown nose
someone who always compliments the boss in order to get ahead

buck stops here
Responsibility is ours, and is not passed on to other people beyond this point

build a better mousetrap
improve a common product

burn the candle at both ends
wake up early, and go to bed late

burn the midnight oil
go to bed late

bury the hatchet
end a fight, make peace

bust your butt
work really hard

by guess or by golly
using a combination of guessing and luck to hit
or miss a target or goal

by hook or by crook
by any means possible

call the shots
to be in charge and make decisions

can't get blood from a turnip
you cannot get something from a person who
does not have the thing you want, usually
referring to money

can't have it both ways
can't satisfy two opposing groups or opinions

can't see for looking
cannot see because you have been looking too long

can't see the forest for the trees
losing sight of the big picture, getting caught in the details

capture the imagination
causing a person to imagine a scene or character

change for the better
something changes or is expected to change that will make things better

change your mind
to change your opinion on something

clean as a whistle
someone who is not involved in anything illegal

collect my thoughts
think calmly and clearly, or to organize one's thoughts

come down off your high horse
stop being so egotistical

come to the point
to get to the important part of something

cover your ass
protect yourself by having documents signed etc.

cross my heart and hope to die
Promise

cross that bridge when I come to it
to not worry about a possible problem until it becomes an actual problem

cup runneth over
feeling too full of love, joy, or happiness

curiousity killed the cat
don't be too curious, leave well enough alone

cut a fine figure
to look very good in your clothes

cut a wide swath
do many things - party, play sports, live, and love

cut the Gordian Knot
to solve a complex problem with a simple solution

dance with the one who brought you
to be loyal to the person who helped you

darken a church door
attend church, got to a church service

did yourself proud
did well, did a good job

different strokes for different folks
people can have different preferences

dig a little deeper
try harder, give a little more

dig in their heels
hold their position, not yield or move

do the honors
do the task for the leader, or to fill in for the leader

do unto others as you would have them do unto you
treat people the way you want to be treated

do your own thing
do it your own way, do it how you feel

do your part
do your share, do your job

do yourself proud
do something that you are proud of

dodge a bullet
avoid a failure, injury, or loss

doing something by the book
doing things precisely as they are meant to be done

dolled up
to dress up in a stylish way

don't bite the hand that feeds you
don't harm someone who has helped you

don't borrow trouble
don't worry about a situation that might never happen

don't bring a knife to a gunfight
don't come unprepared

don't bury your head in the sand
don't ignore something that is obviously
wrong

don't carry coals to Newcastle
don't engage in useless labor

don't carry the weight of the world on your
shoulders
don't be burdened by the problems of the
world

don't change horses in mid-stream
don't change a leader of a group in the middle
of a tough time or controversy

don't come unglued
don't lose control

don't count your chickens before they hatch
don't depend heavily on plans, spend money that you have not received

don't criticize the paint job on the titanic
don't point out petty flaws on something that could not be saved even with a complete overhaul

don't cry over spilt milk
don't cry about small accidents, or to cry instead of doing

don't cut off your nose to spite your face
don't make rash short term choices that hurt your long term goals

<u>don't cut your own throat</u>
don't hurt himself, or be your own worst enemy

<u>don't dig your own grave</u>
don't cause your own failure

<u>don't do it the hard way</u>
don't use a poor method to do something

<u>don't eat that</u>
don't accept that do not believe that

<u>don't flog a dead horse</u>
don't continue to ask or try when there is no hope

<u>don't get mad, get even</u>
don't waste your energy on anger, get even

<u>don't get up on the wrong side of the bed</u>
don't be grouchy or cranky

<u>don't get your tits in a wringer</u>
don't cause trouble for yourself

<u>don't give me any of your lip</u>
don't talk back, do not refuse to do what I ask

<u>don't hold a grudge</u>
don't stay angry for a long time

<u>don't hold your breath</u>
keep your expectations low

<u>don't judge a book by it's cover</u>
don't make judgments based on appearances
alone

<u>don't kill the goose that lays the golden eggs</u>
don't lose or destroy the source of wealth

<u>don't knock it</u>
don't be negative, it could be worse

<u>don't look a gift horse in the mouth</u>
do not be critical of a gift

<u>don't look up a dead horse's ass</u>
don't do a worthless task, a pointless exercise

don't make a mountain out of a molehill
do not cause a big fuss over a small problem

don't make no nevermind
it does not matter, it is not important

don't make waves
do not do anything that will cause problems

don't mince words
don't say nice words when complaining

don't push your luck
don't try to get too much, do not ask for more

<u>don't put all your eggs in one basket</u>
do not invest all of your money in one venture
or company

<u>don't put the cart before the horse</u>
don't do things in the wrong order

<u>don't put too fine a point on</u>
don't be too precise

<u>don't put your foot in your mouth</u>
don't say something that causes pain or
embarrassment

<u>don't rest on your laurels</u>
don't depend only on past success to help you

don't rock the boat
do not cause a change, do not upset anybody

don't rub salt in the wound
don't cause it to be worse, aggravate, or add insult to injury

don't sell yourself short
make sure to mention some of your skills or qualifications

don't sweat it
do not worry about it

don't teach your grandmother how to suck eggs
do not tell me what to do, do not tell me something obvious

don't throw the baby out with the bath water
don't throw away something good with the
waste, don't discard everything

don't wear out your welcome
don't stay or visit too long, or not be welcome
anymore

down to brass tacks
become serious about it

draw a sober breath
be sober, not be drunk

draw attention to
ask people to notice something

draw the line
to stop, or refuse to do it

drive a hard bargain
to pay low price, or to negotiate fairly

drive it home
make a message clear, say it so they can understand

eighty-six it
take it off the list

even a blind pig can find an acorn
if you keep looking and trying, you may succeed

every cloud has a silver lining
every bad thing has its perks

everything old is new again
fashions and trends are repeated again

expand his horizons
experience, discover new ideas

familiarity breeds contempt
a friend may disrespect you if you do not
respect his or her privacy

fend for youself
be independent, care for yourself

fight fire with fire
fight with the same weapon or tactics as your opponent is using

fight tooth and nail
fight hard, fight like an animal

figure out
analyze and understand, discover why

fill the bill
do the job

find fault
to criticize, or look for mistakes

find your voice
discover your own personal style

find your way
find the correct path or way

find yourself
be surprised by what happens to you

fire away
ask questions freely, or comment freely

first come, first served
whoever comes first gets served first

first crack at
first chance to do something

first pancake is always spoiled
the first attempt at a product is usually a failure

fish and company stink after three days
fish should be eaten when its fresh, and guests should not stay long

fish or cut bait
do it instead of talking about it

fly by the seat of your pants
with little money, with little planning

footloose and fancy free
carefree, not committed

from rags to riches
to go from poverty to wealth

full steam ahead
as much power as we have

full strength
not weakened or diluted

garage kept
something kept in good condition

get ahead
to make progress

get along
to cooperate with another person

get around it
to avoid rules or laws

get away with
to not obey the rules, and not get caught

get blood from a stone
to do an impossible task

get busy
begin to work, also can be used in a sexual manner

get down to brass tacks
to become serious about something

get down to business
to work seriously, and not to waste any time
or effort

get in on the ground floor
to be one of the first investors in something, or
to be there at the start

get off a few good ones
tell a few jokes, say a few funny lines

get off your high horse
do not act like you are better than everyone
else

get off your soap box
stop preaching to us

get on your horse
to move, or get started

get revenge
hurt someone who hurt you

get the drop on
start faster

get the green light
get approval to do something

get the hang of
to learn how to do

get the lay of the land
to check the conditions of a situation

get the lead out
to move faster

get the monkey off your back
stop a bad habit of yours

get the picture
to understand something

get the point
understand the idea or message

get the word out
tell the message

get the wrinkles out
improve or revise

get this show on the road
begin to do something

get this straight
understand what is said

get to the bottom of
get the facts, find the cause

get to the point
say what is important

get to the root of the problem
find the cause

get with it
to become aware of something

get your feet wet
attempt it, try it

get your head together
begin to think clearly

get your mind around
to understand something

gild of the lily
decorate a beautiful thing, make a work of art
look even better

give 110%
work harder than required, do more than
asked to do

give a little
to be a little flexible about something

give an arm and a leg
to give a lot, or to pay a lot

give an inch
compromise, or to concede a little bit

give and take
win something and lose something at the same time, negotiate

give her credit
let people know that she helped or contributed

give him a taste of his own medicine
do to him what he does to others

give it all you've got
try very hard at something

give it your best shot
try your hardest at something

give you a run for your money
compete with you, try to defeat you

go against the grain
oppose the natural way of doing something

go along for the ride
to do whatever the other person is doing

go easy on
do not ask him to work hard

go for broke
try your hardest at something

go for the jugular
strike at the vital location

go the distance
finish the race or project

go the extra mile
work longer or harder than expected

go with the flow
do what others do

hang in there
to continue, or to be patient

hang on every word
listen carefully to every word that is said

hang on like grim death
be determined, don't quit

hang tough
continue to try, stay strong and determined

haul ass
do it, hurry, get going

have a ball
enjoy the activity, have a blast, have fun

have a clue
know about the answer, know about the topic

have a soft spot for
have a caring feeling for, have sympathy for, feel for

have the final say
make the final decision, call the shots

hazard a guess
guess at the answer, take a a shot in the dark

he who hesitates is lost
if you hesitate you may not get another chance

hedge your bets
bet safely, bet on two or more horses etc.

hit on all cylinders
running smoothly, operating well, hit it off

hit the books
begin to study, crack a book

hit the ground running
be able to work effectively when you begin a new job, self-starter

hit the nail on the head
say the right word, suggest a good idea

Hobson's choice
accept what is offered or you get nothing;
tight spot

hold water
be logical, be sensible

hold your nose
accept it but not like it, look the other way

hold your own
be equal to the others, keep pace

hold your temper
control your temper, do not lose your temper

hold your tongue
be polite, do not talk back

honesty is the best policy
telling the truth is the best plan, honesty pays off

hunker down
get ready to lift or work, prepare to make an effort

icing on the cake
a bonus, extra benefit, the rest is gravy

if a mussel doesn't open don't eat it
if you force things to happen you may regret it, leave well enough alone

if you can't stand the heat, get out of the kitchen
if you do not like the pressure you can leave; if you can't cut it, you can't stay

if you're born to hang, you won't drown
fate controls how we die; we do not control the time and cause of our death

ignorance is bliss
ignorant people have nothing to worry about

in control
able to manage

in her good graces
being liked by her, doing what she likes

it ain't over till it's over
a game is not finished until time has expired, never say die

it ain't over till the fat lady sings
an event is not finished until the final bell, don't give up

it don't make no nevermind
it does not matter, it is not important, never mind

it goes with the territory
some problems are natural in some jobs or places

it goes without saying
it is obvious, needless to say

<u>*it is better to have loved and lost than never to have loved at all*</u>

you are a better person if you have loved someone - even for a short time

<u>*it takes one to know one*</u>

one type of personality recognizes the same type

<u>*it takes two to tango*</u>

some things you cannot do alone; you need a friend to experience life; two can share, fight, dance, love...; it is better to have loved and lost...

<u>*it's a jungle out there*</u>

the world is dangerous, the world is cruel

it's a whole other world out there
it is very different in that place, it is strange
over there

it's a zoo in there
it is a crazy place, it is a wild party, it's a jungle
out there

it's as plain as the nose on your face
very easy to see or understand, very clear,
crystal clear

jack of all trades
a person who has many skills

jump at the chance
be ready to try if you have the opportunity

jump in with both feet
become totally involved, go whole hog

keep a promise
do what you promise to do

keep a secret
not tell anyone, keep it to yourself

keep a stiff upper lip
do not cry, do not be afraid

keep a straight face
not smile or laugh, have a a poker face

keep an even keel
be steady, be calm and sensible

keep an open mind
be fair to all opinions, avoid prejudging

keep the ball rolling
continue the work, encourage us to continue

keep the wolf from the door
keep us fed, prevent hunger

keep up the good work
continue to do good work, 'at a boy

keep your eyes on the clouds on the horizon
watch for problems or events you think will happen in the future

keep your eyes peeled
look or watch carefully, watch for

keep your nose to the grindstone
continue to work hard

kick at the cat
a turn, a try, have a go

kick some ass
win, beat the other team, show them who is the best

kill an elephant
do too much, do ten times more than necessary, overdo it

kill ourselves laughing
laugh hard, hoot, split a gut

kill two birds with one stone
get two with one try, do two jobs on one trip

knock the wind out of his sails
cause him to slow down, cause him to quit,
knock him down a peg

know the ropes
know how, have much experience, learn the
ropes

know the score
know what is happening, in the know, know
your stuff

know where we stand
know our position, know if we have a chance,
leave me hanging

know which end is up
know where you are, know what to do next

know which side your bread is buttered on
know who pays your salary, If you refuse extra
work, you have common sense, bite the hand
that feeds...

know your stuff
know a lot, know facts, have the answers

know your way around
know how to survive, be worldly wise

knuckle down
work harder, achieve more

land on your feet
be ready to work, be ready for action, hit the ground running

lead a life
have a style of living, have a way of life

learn the lingo
learn the language, know the idioms

learn the ropes
learn the first steps, learn the basics, know the ropes

learn your place
learn to know where and when to speak

leave no stone unturned
look everywhere, look high and low

leave the door open
allow people to reply, invite a response, feel
free to reply

leave well enough alone
if you do more you could cause more trouble

let sleeping dogs lie
do not create problems, leave things alone

let the chips fall where they may
let it happen naturally, do not control everything

let the good times roll
let the party begin, let us enjoy our time together, the more the merrier

life is just a bowl of cherries
life is just wonderful, life is grand

life is not all guns and roses
life is not all war and love, life is not like the movies

look out for number one
help yourself first, get enough for yourself

look over your shoulder
look to see who is following you

make a clean breast of it
tell all you know about it, admit what you did

make a comeback
try to recover your former skill and success,
comeback kid

make a difference
affect or change it, tip the scales

make a life for yourself
live a good life; have a job, home and family

make a living
earn enough money to live on, make your way

make hay while the sun shines
work while the weather is good, work while
we have time and helpers

make something of yourself
be successful, be respected for your skill and
honesty

make the grade
do acceptable work, measure up

make the most of it
do the best you can, seize the opportunity

make the team
become a member of the team

make tracks
hurry, move quickly, vamoose

make your bum hum
excite you, please your senses, turn you on

make your mark
be known for an invention or an achievement,
set the world on fire

mend fences
solve political problems, listen to voters

mind over matter
believing you can do it, using the mind's power

mind your manners
be polite, be courteous, watch your P's and Q's

mind your own business
do not ask questions about my business

mind your P's and Q's
be polite, do not drink too much, mind your manners

money doesn't grow on trees
money is not easy to get, we value our money

money is the root of all evil
money is the cause of bad things

mount a comeback
begin to score goals or points while losing,
snatch victory from...

move your ass
move quickly, get going, move it

Murphy's Law
"Anything that can go wrong will go wrong."

necessity is the mother of invention
our needs cause us to invent devices

never say die
never quit, never give up

nip it in the bud
stop it before it grows, prevent it from spreading

no rest for the wicked
wicked people must work long hours as a penalty

nothing succeeds like success
one success leads to more success

nothing to sneeze at
of good quality, do not ignore it

nothing ventured, nothing gained
if you try nothing, you will gain nothing

on my best behavior
being polite to everyone, behaving in an appropriate manner

on schedule
within the dates on the plan, on target

on the double
quickly, now, move it

on the up and up
legal, within the law, not underhanded

on your guard
careful, cautious

on your toes
ready, alert

one born every minute
many easy customers, lots of suckers

one man's garbage is another man's art
each person has different likes and dislikes, to each his own

one man's meat is another man's poison
one person likes what another person hates, to each his own

open some doors
provide opportunities, help someone succeed

outdo yourself
perform better than before, do your personal best

paddle your own canoe
be an individual, be independent

paint a picture
describe in detail, portray with words

paint the town red
have a party downtown, go out on the town

pay my respects
attend a ceremony or send a symbol of your respect for someone

pay the penalty
pay a fine, endure, receive punishment

pay the price
work hard, endure, suffer

pay tribute
show that you respect or admire a person, honor someone

pay your dues
work hard and learn, be loyal for years

pay your way
pay your share of the expenses

people who live in glass houses shouldn't throw stones
people who have faults should not criticize others

play fair
play using rules, give everyone an equal chance

play hardball
play tough, try to hurt the opponent

play it safe
be careful, do not take a chance

pound the pavement
look for a job, walk from company to company to find a job

practice what you preach
do what you say people should do

prepare like crazy
prepare thoroughly, be ready for an event or test

pride goeth before a fall
you lose self-respect before you do an evil deed

pull in your horns
not be so aggressive, stop attacking or criticizing

pull out all the stops
work as hard as possible

pull punches
talk nice, ease up, take it easy on you

pull yourself together
control your sadness, get a grip on yourself

push the boat out
work harder to complete the job, give 110%,
go the extra mile

push the right buttons
say the right things, do the right things

put in a hard day
work hard all day, a hard day

put out of its misery
kill because it is suffering, put down

put the finishing touches on
add the last details or trimmings

put the hammer down
go faster, floor it, pedal to the metal

put the right spin on it
say it in a diplomatic way, bafflegab, doctor it,
spin doctor

put things in perspective
see things as they are, see the actual size

put to rest
not think or worry about it any more

put your best foot forward
try to do your best work, present yourself well

put your heart into it
try hard, do your best, give it your best shot

put your money where your mouth is
pay what you offered, put up or shut up

put your shoulder to the wheel
begin to work

put yourself through college
earn money to pay for your college education

read between the lines
see what is not written, read the implied message, find the hidden meaning

realize your potential
be the best you can, come into your own

ride the wave
use luck or success to achieve more success

run the gamut
look at what is available, check the range of choices

run the gauntlet
run past the enemy, go through a dangerous area

save for a rainy day
save money for a time when you really need it

save your bacon
save you from failure or disaster

save your skin/neck
save you from risk, dismissal or death

seize the opportunity
act now to gain most, take advantage of

shit or get off the pot
do it or move, dog in the manger

sleep in
sleep until late in the morning

sleep it off
sleep until you are sober, sleep until you feel normal

sleep like a log
sleep well, sleep soundly, dead to the world, deep sleep

smooth out
solve a problem or argument

so far, so good
doing fine this far, good this far

sober up
become sober, wait until you are not drunk

soften up
cause a person to be more cooperative

soften your stance
cause you to change your opinion or position

soldier on
continue working; serving well

sometimes life is a bucket of shit and the handle is inside
sometimes life is very unpleasant, life is not all guns and roses

speak up
speak louder, crank it up

speak your mind
say what you think or feel, speak out

speed up
go faster, accelerate

stand for
believe in and represent, be the symbol for

stand out
appear different, not be the same as the others

stand up and be counted
say you support and will vote for it, stand up for

stand up for
support, protect, speak out for

stay abreast
be aware of developments, stay current, keep pace

stay alive
win enough to continue, continue in a series

stay awake
not sleep, be alert

stay busy as a beaver
stay very busy

stay in line
obey the rules, behave well

steal the show
be the favorite performer, receive the most applause

stretch the dollar
spend carefully, buy the most for each dollar

stretch the envelope
extend the boundaries, expand your horizons

strike a bargain
find a satisfactory deal or price

strike it rich
earn or win a lot of money, find a gold mine

strike up a conversation
begin a conversation with a stranger

strike while the iron is hot
do it before it is too late, now is the time to act

swallow your pride
do not let your pride stop you, control your pride

take a load off your feet
sit down, grab a chair, have a seat

take action
act in a deliberate way, act with a purpose

take by storm
rush in, win by force, overwhelm

take care of
care for someone or something, look after

<u>take care of business</u>
do what needs to be done, do my job

<u>take chances</u>
live dangerously, risk something valuable, play with fire

<u>take charge</u>
be in control, supervise

<u>take cover</u>
hide, find a safe place

<u>take five</u>
rest for five minutes, take a break

take it with a grain of salt
do not believe all of it, some of it is not true

take solace
find peace, find comfort

take the bull by the horns
control the problem, be firm, take charge

take time to smell the roses
use some time to relax and enjoy the scenery

take your lumps
endure bumps and hits, suffer through injuries

take your sweet time
you are too slow, you could work faster, pick up the pace

take your time
do not rush, do it when you have enough time, no rush

take your turn
act or speak when your name is called, it's your turn

talk is cheap
talk is not action, saying is easier than doing

that's all she wrote
that is the end of the story, there is no more

that's the spirit
good work, good attitude, way to go

that's the way the ball bounces
that is fate, that's life

that's the way the cookie crumbles
that is fate, that is the way things happen

the apple doesn't fall far from the tree
kids are like their parents; a chip off the old block; like father, like son

the ball's in your court
you speak or act now, it's your turn

<u>the best-laid plans of mice and men go oft astray</u>
plans are not guaranteed, plans sometimes do not work out

<u>the bigger they are the harder they fall</u>
we can beat the big guys, big players fall harder, mind over matter

<u>the blind leading the blind</u>
the leader is ignorant or incompetent

<u>the devil makes work for idle hands</u>
if a person is not busy he will do evil things, work ethic

<u>the early bird gets the worm</u>
the one who arrives first gets the reward

the end justifies the means
any method is fine if the result is good

the first pancake is always spoiled
the first attempt or product is usually a failure

The Golden Rule
Do unto others as you would have them do unto you.

the Lord helps those who help themselves
if you work to help yourself God will help you

the more the merrier
if more people come, we will have a better party

<u>the past is slipping by without a trace</u>
in order to have a significant past we need to create a significant present; the present is the past and vice versa

<u>the proof of the pudding is in the eating</u>
do not judge until you test the finished product, do not jump to conclusions

<u>the road to hell is paved with good intentions</u>
good intentions achieve nothing without action, actions speak louder...

<u>the squeaky wheel gets the grease</u>
the person who complains loudest gets service

the way to a man's heart is through his stomach
feeding a man good food will cause him to love you, beauty is only skin deep

there are two sides to every story
two people tell different stories of the same event, compare notes

there is nothing either good or bad, but thinking makes it so
nothing is good or bad in and of itself; humans impose their morality on objects, actions and events

there's many a slip twixt the cup and the lip
it is easy to spill what you are drinking; it is easy to make mistakes

there's more than meets the eye
part of the story has not been told

there's more than one way to skin a cat
there are many ways to do it, I know another
method

there's one born every minute
there are lots of people who will believe
anything, there are lots of suckers

think outside the box
think in new ways, imagine, big-sky thinking,
think tank

think straight
think clearly, be rational

through thick and thin
during good and bad times, for better or worse

throw caution to the wind
live or act carelessly, not be cautious

tie up loose ends
finish a project, complete the details of some work, finishing touch

time flies when you're having fun
time goes quickly when you are playing, how time flies

to each his own
we like different things

<u>too many chiefs and not enough Indians</u>
too many directors and not enough workers,
too many cooks...

<u>too many cooks spoil the broth</u>
too many managers cause problems

<u>try your darndest</u>
try very hard, bend over backwards, go the
extra mile

<u>try your hand at</u>
try to do, try it

<u>try your luck</u>
see if you can win, you take a chance

turn about is fair play
you get what you give, what goes around...

two heads are better than one
listen to more than one opinion

two's company, three's a crowd
two people are happier than three, the third person is not welcome

variety is the spice of life
a variety of experiences makes life interesting, to each his own

wake up and smell the coffee
be more aware

wake with a start
wake suddenly, jump out of bed

wash your hands of it
not be involved anymore, withdraw from a
project

wasn't born yesterday
wise from experience, been around

watch over like a mother hawk
watch carefully and protect, keep an eye on

watch your language
do not swear, do not use crude language

watch your P's and Q's
be polite, mind your manners

watch your step
watch where you step, be careful

water under the bridge
the past, history

wear your heart on your sleeve
show your emotions, reveal your true feelings

weather the storm
survive a crisis, live through tough times

what you don't know won't hurt you
if you do not know about a problem, you do not worry

what's good for the goose is good for the gander
rules that apply to the wife also apply to the husband, tit for tat

when in Rome, do as the Romans do
when you are a visitor do the same things as your hosts do

when it rains it pours
when it comes we get too much, feast or famine

where the rubber hits the road
where the theory is tested, when the action begins; the nitty-gritty

where there's a will, there's a way
when we are determined we find a way to succeed, when the going gets tough

winning isn't everything; it's the only thing
winning is the only thing that matters, get it straight

work it out
solve it, try to agree

work things out
discuss a problem and find a solution, work it out

work your ass off
work very hard, work my buns off

worship the ground she walks on
love her very, very much; crawl on my hands...,
mad about her

wouldn't say shit if her mouth was full of it
would not say a bad word, would not swear

you can lead a horse to water but you can't
make him drink
you can provide what they need but you
cannot force them to use it

you can run but you can't hide
you can run away but you cannot hide from
your past or your problems

<u>you can thank your lucky stars</u>
you were lucky, be thankful you are safe

<u>you can't make a silk purse out of a sow's ear</u>
you cannot improve the quality of junk; cannot make gold from iron

<u>you can't sell anybody if you don't love everybody</u>
you will be more successful if you have love in your heart

<u>you can't teach an old dog new tricks</u>
old dogs and old people do not like to change or learn, die hard

you can't tell a book by its cover
the cover or surface does not reveal its
contents, beauty is only skin deep

you don't miss the water till the well runs dry
you do not appreciate some things until they
go away or become extinct

you have to be good to be lucky
people with ability cause their own good luck

you need money to make money
you have to spend money to make a profit,
nothing succeeds like...

you reap whatsoever you sow
you will see the long-term effects of your
actions, chickens come home...

<u>you snooze, you lose</u>

if you are not alert you will lose an opportunity, seize the opportunity

<u>you're only as good as your last shift</u>

you are judged by your most recent work, don't rest on your laurels